NEW WA

Fat
birthday
and other stories

The sports day page 3

Fat Pig's birthday page 10

Lots of caps page 17

M

Macmillan Education

Editorial Consultant: Donna Bailey
The publishers would like to thank the following
for their stories:
Diana Perkins for The sports day, illustrated by Elizabeth Haines.
Penny Hegarty for Fat Pig's birthday, illustrated by Nina O'Connell.
Jean Chapman for Lots of caps, illustrated by Tony Kenyon.

First published 1987
Reprinted 1987, 1988

Published by
MACMILLAN EDUCATION LTD
Houndmills, Basingstoke, Hampshire RG21 2XS
and London
Companies and representatives
throughout the world

Cover design by The Design Works, Reading

Printed in Hong Kong

British Library Cataloguing in Publication Data
New Way level 2
(Basic reader)
1. Readers—1950-
I. Series
428.6 PE1119
ISBN 0-333-38395-8

The sports day

I have a sack, said Tom.
I am in a race.
I am in the sack race.

I have a big sack.
I will jump in my sack.
I will go fast.

I am in a race.

I am in the sack race, said Jenny.

I will jump in my sack.

It is time for the race.
Tom is in his sack.
Jenny is in her sack.

One, two, three, go,
said Tom's Dad.
Jump as fast as you can.

Tom was in front.
He fell over.
Jenny went past.
Tom got up.
He went very fast.

Hello Tom, said his Dad.
You have jumped fast but
you have jumped back
to the start.

Fat Pig's birthday

It is Fat Pig's birthday.
I will have a party,
said Fat Pig.

Don’t forget to come
to my party, said Fat Pig.
We will not forget,
said Meg and Ben.
We will not forget,
said Jip and Sam.

It is my birthday,
said Fat Pig to Deb.
Don't forget to come
to my party.

I will put a knot
in my tail, said Deb.
Then I will not forget.

Deb put a big knot
in her tail.
I will not forget
the party now, said Deb.

Jip and Meg came
to the party.
Sam and Ben came
to the party.

Deb came to the party.
She had a knot in her tail.
Look, I did not forget
to come to the party, said Deb.

Lots of caps

A man had ten caps for sale.
He put all the caps on top
of his head.
Caps for sale. Caps for sale,
he said.
Big caps. Little caps.
Caps for sale.
No one came to get a cap.

The man sat down by a tree.

He was hot, so hot.

He went to sleep.

Zzzzzzz. Zzzzzzz. Zzzzzzz.

When he woke up
he had one cap on his head,
but that was all.
He looked and looked
for his caps.

Ttt. Ttt. Ttt. Ttt.
The man looked up.
Lots of monkeys sat in the tree.
Give me my caps, said the man.
Ttt. Ttt, said the monkeys and
they clapped their hands.

Give me my caps,
said the man and
he stamped his feet.
Ttt. Ttt, said the monkeys and
they stamped their feet.

The man was cross.
He took off his cap and
threw it down.
The monkeys took off their
caps and threw them down.

So the man put on his cap.

He put all the caps on to his head.

Caps for sale.

Caps for sale, he said.

He went down the road.
Big caps. Little caps.
Caps for sale.
Ttt. Ttt, said the monkeys
in the tree.
Ttt. Ttt. Ttt. Ttt.